Note to Parents and Teachers

The READING ABOUT: STARTERS series introduces key science vocabulary to young children while encouraging them to discover and understand the world around them. The series works as a set of graded readers in three levels.

LEVEL 2: BEGIN TO READ ALONE follows guidelines set out in the National Curriculum for Year 2 in schools. These books can be read alone or as part of guided or group reading. Each book has three sections:

• Information pages that introduce key words. These key words appear in bold for easy recognition on pages where the related science concepts are explained.
• A lively story that recalls this vocabulary and encourages children to use these words when they talk and write.
• A quiz and index ask children to look back and recall what they have read.

Questions for Further Investigation

TRACTORS explains key concepts about FORCES. Here are some suggestions for further discussion linked to the questions on the information spreads:

p. 5 *Which is stronger or quicker, a tractor or a cart horse?* Ask children to think about how we could test which of the two is faster or stronger.

p. 7/9 *What other things do you pull/push to make them move?* Ask children to think about both big movements, such as pushing a swing or tug-of-war, and small movements such as typing or playing an instrument. Children could also mime different actions.

p. 11 *What shapes can you make with clay using pushes and pulls?* Children can make shapes by twisting, stretching etc. Ask them to say whether actions are pushes or pulls.

p. 13 *What machines use fuel, electricity or wind to work?* Trucks or cars use fuel; smaller machines use electricity, e.g. CD player, mobile phone; sailing boats use wind.

p. 15 *How would you slow down on a scooter that has no brakes?* You could introduce the idea of friction, e.g. using feet to slow down on a scooter or on a slide.

p. 17 *How hard would it be to move a car without wheels?* Ask children to experiment using pencils under a stack of books to see how wheels help to move heavy objects.

p. 19 *How do you steer a bike or a scooter?* By turning the handlebars. You could also ask children to think about how they make other machines turn, e.g. sledge, skateboard.

p. 21 *When a toy rolls on different surfaces, how can you measure how far it has gone?* Ask children to measure using a rule and non-standard measures, such as straws.

ADVISORY TEAM

Educational Consultant
Andrea Bright – Science Co-ordinator, Trafalgar Junior School, Twickenham

Literacy Consultant
Jackie Holderness – former Senior Lecturer in Primary Education, Westminster Institute, Oxford Brookes University

Series Consultants
Anne Fussell – Early Years Teacher and University Tutor, Westminster Institute, Oxford Brookes University

David Fussell – C.Chem., FRSC

CONTENTS

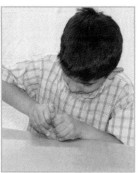

4   tractor, work, cab

6   pull, machine, plough

8   push, bulldozer

10   force, lift, dig

12   engine, fuel

14   fast, accelerator, slow, brakes

16   wheel, roll, axle

18   turn, steer, direction, gears

20   surface, soft, hard

22   tyre, tread, grip, slip, stud

24   **Story: Tractor to the Rescue!**
Can Josie save the sheep?

31   **Quiz**

32   **Index**

© Aladdin Books Ltd 2005

Designed and produced by
Aladdin Books Ltd
2/3 Fitzroy Mews
London W1T 6DF

First published in
Great Britain in 2005 by
Franklin Watts
96 Leonard Street
London EC2A 4XD

A catalogue record for this book is available from the British Library.

ISBN 0 7496 6243 3

Printed in Malaysia

All rights reserved

Editor: Jim Pipe

Design: Flick, Book Design and Graphics

Thanks to:
• The pupils of Trafalgar Infants School, Twickenham for appearing as models in this book.
• Sophie and Alex Stephens for appearing as models in the story, and to Eric and Jane Jedwab for organising the shoot.
• The pupils and teachers of Trafalgar Junior School, Twickenham and St. Nicholas C.E. Infant School, Wallingford, for testing the sample books.

Photocredits:
l-left, r-right, b-bottom, t-top, c-centre, m-middle
Cover tl, 20t — Stockbyte. Cover tc & tr, 2tl, 3, 9b, 11t, 13t, 14b, 17 both, 31 ml, 31mr, 31bl, 31br — John Deere. Cover b, 4, 7b, 10b, 12b, 15t, 16b, 18b, 22b, 31tr, 31bc, 32 — Renault. 2ml, 7t, 10tr, 11b, 21 both — PBD. 2bl, 8br, 16tr, 23l — Corbis. 5tl — Corel. 5b — USDA. 6tl, 12tr —Comstock. 6b, 18m — Bill Tarpenning/USDA. 8t, 9tr, 19br, 28tr — Photodisc. 13br, 14tr — Brand X Pictures. 15br, 22tr — Jim Pipe. 19tr — Digital Vision. 19ml, 23 top right — Select Pictures. 20br — Eyewire (Photodisc). 24-30 all (except 28tr) — Eric Jedwab.

Starters

FORCES

Tractors

by Sally Hewitt

Aladdin/Watts
London • Sydney

Tractors are strong, powerful machines. They have huge wheels and big engines.

Tractors do heavy **work** on the farm. The driver sits in the **cab**. Inside the **cab** are controls to drive the **tractor**.

Cab

Some farmers use oxen instead of a tractor.

Before **tractors** were invented, farmers used big cart horses to do heavy **work**.

The horses pulled farm machines and carts loaded with hay.

• Which is stronger or quicker, a tractor or a cart horse?

Tractors **pull** big farm **machines**. **Machines** make work easier.

A **plough** is a farm **machine**. The driver attaches **machines** to the tractor.

You can make a cart move when you pull it.

The tractor moves forwards and **pulls** the **plough** along behind it.

A **plough** digs up the earth. What would you use to dig up the earth?

Plough

Pushing is the opposite to pulling.

You pull things towards you. You **push** things away from you.

You **push** a toy car to move it along. You **push** keys on a keyboard.

8

A tractor is used to **push** as well as pull.

A **bulldozer** blade is attached to the front of the tractor.

The tractor moves forwards and **pushes** earth or snow away.

Bulldozer

When you jump, you push your feet against the ground.

• What other things do you push to make them move?

Pushes and pulls are **forces**.
Forces make things move.

A loader on the front
of a tractor can pull
straw up to **lift** it.

A heavy load of straw
needs a big **force** to **lift** it.

You pull to lift
up a bag.

The loader bucket pushes into the earth. It **lifts** the earth out to **dig** a hole.

You use **forces** to make a clay model.

You push and squash and pull and stretch it.

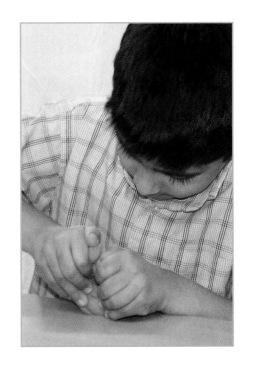

• What shapes can you make with clay using pushes or pulls?

A tractor **engine** is bigger than a car **engine**.

The **engine** makes a strong force. It turns the wheels.

When the wheels turn, they push the tractor along.

You move along when your muscles pull your bones.

Engine

Fuel gives things the energy they need to work.

Fuel gives a tractor **engine** energy to move the wheels.

Food is the **fuel** that gives you energy to work.

• What machines use electricity, fuel or wind to work?

To go **faster**, a tractor driver pushes the **accelerator**.

This gives the engine more power.
The wheels turn **faster**.

The wheels push the ground, so the tractor goes **faster**.

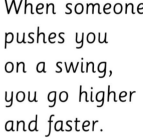

When someone pushes you on a swing, you go higher and faster.

14

To **slow** down and stop, the tractor driver pushes the **brake** pedal.

The **brakes** push against the wheels. The tractor goes **slower**.

The **brakes** on a bike push against the wheels, too. The bike **slows** down and then stops.

• How would you slow down on a scooter that has no brakes?

Tractors, cars, bikes and skates use **wheels** to **roll** along the ground.

A tractor has huge back **wheels** and smaller front **wheels**.

Wheels are round. A round shape turns very easily.

Do you think square wheels would work?

Wheels

Each **wheel** is fixed
to the end of an **axle**.

An **axle** is a rod
that can turn around.

Axle

There are **axles** for the back
and front **wheels** of a tractor.

• How hard would it be to move a car without wheels?

The tractor driver **turns** the **steering** wheel to change **direction**. The driver can **steer** straight or **turn** left or right.

Steering wheel

Gear lever

The driver changes **gear** to make the tractor go forwards or backwards.

How do you make
things change **direction**?

You **steer** a bumper car.

You push or pull
a toy tractor to
make it go forwards
or backwards.

You hit a
tennis ball to
make it change
direction.

• How do you steer a bike or a scooter?

A **surface** can make things go faster or slower.

A tractor often has to drive over a **surface** of **soft** mud.

The wheels sink into the **soft** mud and the tractor slows down.

Your feet sink into soft sand.

20

Wood has a **hard**, smooth **surface**.
A carpet has a bumpy **surface**.

Roll a toy car or tractor down a slope.
The toy rolls further over smooth wood
than over **soft** carpet.

Wood

Carpet

• When a toy rolls on different surfaces, how can you measure how far it has gone?

The **tyres** on a tractor's wheels have a deep pattern. This is the **tread**.

The **tread grips** the ground beneath the mud.

The **tread** stops the tractor from **slipping**.

Feel the bumps and hollows on a bicycle tyre. This is the tread.

Studs

Football boots have **studs** on the soles.

The **studs** work like the **tread** of a tractor **tyre**.

The **studs grip** the ground. They stop a footballer from **slipping** over in the mud.

• How do your trainers grip the ground? Take a look!

TRACTOR TO THE RESCUE!

Look out for words about **forces**.

It had been raining on the farm all day.

"I wish the rain would stop," grumbled Josie.

The kitchen door burst open and Dad came in. "We must rescue the sheep from the bottom field," he said.

"The field may flood in all this rain. I'll take the **tractor** and trailer".

"I'll help," said Mum.
"So will I!" said Josie.

"Put on your boots,"
said Dad. "You could
slip in the **soft** mud."

Dad attached the trailer to
the **tractor**. "I'll drive," said Mum.

Mum climbed into the driver's **cab**
and turned on the **engine**.

The **tractor** moved forwards **slowly**,
pulling the trailer behind it.

Dad whistled and Rory the sheep dog ran up.

Dad, Josie and Rory followed the **tractor**. "Go **faster**, Mum," shouted Josie.

"No," said Dad.

"When the **wheels turn slowly**, the **tyres grip** the ground and the **tractor** doesn't **slip**."

"Go **slower**, Mum, use the **brakes!**" shouted Josie. Dad laughed.

The sky grew darker.
The rain grew heavier.
"Poor sheep!"
said Josie.

Dad **pushed** open
the farmyard gate.

Mum **steered**
the **tractor** into
the field.

Josie **pulled** the gate
shut. She ran back to
Dad and nearly **slipped**
over in the mud.

Mum stopped the **tractor** and looked out of the **cab**.

"The **tread** on the **tyres** may not **grip** this muddy slope," she said.

"We'll put straw over the mud so the **surface** is less slippery."

Dad, Mum and Josie **worked fast**. They could hear the sheep bleating.

Mum drove the **tractor slowly** down the slope.

The **tyres gripped** the straw and the **tractor** didn't **slip**.

"Look! The field is flooding," said Josie. "We're just in time!"

Mum **turned** the **tractor** round. She changed **gear** and drove the **tractor** backwards. The **tractor pushed** the trailer into position.

Rory ran in all **directions** and rounded up the sheep. Dad **pulled** down the back of the trailer.

The sheep ran into the trailer. Mum and Dad **lifted** up the back of the trailer.

The **tractor pulled** the trailer back to the farmyard.

"Great! Now all the sheep are safe!" said Josie.

Think about your day. How many different **pushes** and **pulls** do you make? Write them down in a list or draw them. Or draw a picture of a **tractor pushing** or **pulling**.

I lift the bucket.

The tractor pulls a trailer.

QUIZ

Why do **tractors**
need an **engine**?

Answer on page 12

What gives a **tractor**
engine energy to work?

Answer on page 13

How do **tyres grip**
slippery ground?

Answer on page 22

What are these tractors doing?
What forces are they using?

Have you read this book? Well done! Do you remember these words? Look back and find out.

INDEX

A
accelerator 14
axle 16

B
brakes 14
bulldozer 8

C
cab 4

D
dig 10
direction 18

E
engine 12

F
fast 14
force 10
fuel 12

G
gears 18
grip 22

H
hard 20

L
lift 10

M
machine 6

P
plough 6
pull 6
push 8

R
roll 16

S
slip 22

slow 14
soft 20
steer 18
stud 22
surface 20

T
tractor 4
tread 22
turn 18
tyre 22

W
wheel 16
work 4